DIY Projects & Gift Ideas for Summer

By: Do It Yourself Nation

Copyright © 2015 by Do It Yourself Nation

All rights reserved. No part of this book may be reproduced in any form without permission in writing from the author. Reviewers are able to quote brief passages in reviews.

Disclaimer

This document is geared towards providing exact and reliable information in regards to the topic and issue covered. The publication is sold with the idea that the publisher is not required to render accounting, officially permitted, or otherwise, qualified services. If advice is necessary, legal or professional, a practiced individual in the profession should be ordered.

- *From a Declaration of Principles which was accepted and approved equally by a Committee of the American Bar Association and a Committee of Publishers and Associations.*

In no way is it legal to reproduce, duplicate, or transmit any part of this document in either electronic means or in printed format. Recording of this publication is strictly prohibited and any storage of this document is not allowed unless with written permission from the publisher. All rights reserved.

The information provided herein is stated to be truthful and consistent, in that any liability, in terms of inattention or otherwise, by any usage or abuse of any policies, processes, or directions contained within is the solitary and utter responsibility of the recipient reader. Under no circumstances will any legal responsibility or blame be held against the publisher for any reparation, damages, or monetary loss due to the information herein, either directly or indirectly.

Respective authors own all copyrights not held by the publisher.

The information herein is offered for informational purposes solely, and is universal as so. The presentation of the information is without contract or any type of guarantee assurance.

The trademarks that are used are without any consent, and the publication of the trademark is without permission or backing by the trademark owner. All trademarks and brands within this book are for clarifying purposes only and are the owned by the owners themselves, not affiliated with this document.

Introduction

As you prepare to study this book, take some time to reflect on the following:

It's summertime and you find it hard to decide what gifts to offer your loved ones. You've probably been giving gifts all year round for various occasions, but for summer you want something different. Do you find it challenging to come up with a unique gift every summer? Have you been spending lots of money buying very expensive gifts? Do you want a break from all that? Did you know that handmade gifts are quite inexpensive and are likely to leave a lasting impression?

The book is especially to help you express your love to your friends, family, coworkers, and other people in your life this summer. It is well illustrated with colorful images highlighting simple and doable steps for making unique handmade gifts.

Read on and get amazing ideas on how to make the best gifts for summer.

About This Book

This book is sub-divided into four chapters which discus various categories of DIY gifts in detail as follows:

- The first chapter suggests some of the easiest home décor gifts to make or design this summer.
- The second chapter illustrates ways of making amazing accessories and crafts.
- The third chapter describes how to make some amazing food gifts.
- Finally, the last chapter has other miscellaneous gifts you can give this summer.

Refer to the table of contents to help you find your way through the book.

Table of Contents

Introduction — 3

About This Book — 4

Chapter 1: Home Décor Gifts — 7
- DIY Vertical Plant Hanger — 7
- Fabric Covered Spring Vases — 12
- Framed Key Specimen Art — 14
- Reupholster a chair — 17
- DIY Faux Headboard — 19
- DIY Fabric Art — 21

Chapter 2: Homemade Crafts, Clothes and Accessories — 23
- Reusable Lunch Bags — 23
- DIY Mason Jar Soap Pump — 27
- Mason Jar Cozies — 28
- Mesh beach bag — 31
- Simple hair bow tutorial — 34

Chapter 3: Summer Food Gifts — 35
- Decadent Brownie Pie — 35
- Mint Chocolate Cake — 37
- Creamy Garlic Mushrooms — 40

Chapter 4: Miscellaneous Summer Gifts — 42
- Cute button bookmarks — 42
- Homemade Sandcastle Kit — 43
- Bubble solution and blowers — 44

Conclusion — 46

Key Takeaways from this Book	47
How to Put This Information into Action	48
Here's another book you might like:	49
Preview of DIY Projects & Gift Ideas for Easter:	50
More Books You Might Like	59
Your Free Bonus	60

Chapter 1: Home Décor Gifts

DIY Vertical Plant Hanger

What you'll need

Paint and/or stain

Sandpaper

Jigsaw

Drill and 3/8" bit

Metal ring

Rope

Plants

Terra cotta pots

Scrap wood

How to make

Place a pot upside down on wood, then measure and mark a square around your pot. Ensure that you leave a one-inch border on the sides. Cut the square using a chop saw.

In the center of the square, trace the top of the pot in order to create a hole for the pot to sit in. Then mark and draw another circle, ¼ inch smaller, inside the initial circle.

Drill a hole through the smaller circle using the 3/8" drill bit. This will allow you to fit the jigsaw blade inside. Cut around the circle using a jigsaw to have the piece pop out. By now, the pot should be able to fit into the wood square.

In each corner of the square, use the 3/8" bit to drill a hole where your rope can thread through. Remove wood splinters from the square using sandpaper. When done, stain or paint the square your desired color.

You may also choose to apply a whitish chalk paint to your pot to make it brighter and still leave the terra cotta showing underneath, especially if you used a dark walnut stain for the wood.

When you're finished painting, start to assemble your hanger. You can use any number of pots and squares; just adjust the dimensions as desired.

Now cut out four 6-foot pieces of rope and then thread them through the holes you made in one of the wood squares. Tie a knot underneath each hole to hold the rope in place. This first square will form the bottom piece.

To add another piece, make a knot in each of the ropes at about 10-12 inches above the last knot. Then add the next wood square and slide it down to these new knots. Just repeat the procedure to add more pieces. Remember to make sure they're sitting level!

For indoor use, attach the bottom piece to the last pot so you don't get your floor wet when you water them (you may need some superglue to join the two pieces). Otherwise, just put paper coffee filters in the bottom of the pots before adding soil so that water can drip through. Now add some plants; succulents and flowers look particularly attractive in these hangers.

Hang the planter by pulling the top of the rope pieces through a metal ring. Then secure by wrapping either a floral wire or a tight knot around the rope.

Fabric Covered Spring Vases

What you'll need

Hot glue gun

Glue sticks

Recycled bottles

Twine

Sewing pins

Paint brush

Craft paint

Painter's tape

Plain fabric or drop cloth

How to make

Start by cutting a 10x10" square of fabric for every 12-ounce bottle you'll use. To create stripes, add a few strips of painter's tape over the fabric. You can either eyeball them or measure them out. Make sure to press down the edges properly so the paint doesn't seep out.

Between the tapes, paint the fabric using your preferred colors. You can try out yellow, pink and light green for a nice spring décor. When done, remove the tape. Completely dry the painted piece of fabric before proceeding.

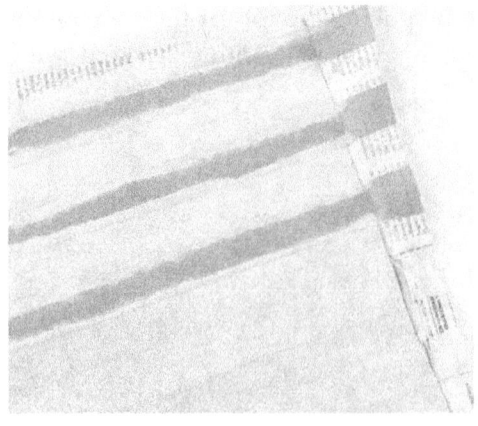

When the paint has dried, wrap the fabric squares around the bottles. Ensure that the fabric is wrapped snug around the largest part of the bottle then pin it in place.

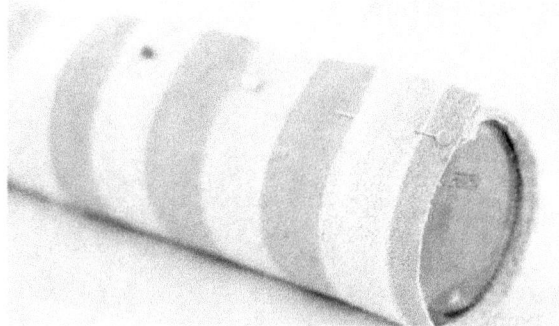

Add some hot glue to one edge of the fabric, and then press it onto the other edge. Leave the pins in place as you do this. After the glue has set, remove the pins and use twine to tie a bow to cinch the top of the vase. Add your favorite flowers; tulips are nice here.

Framed Key Specimen Art

What you'll need

Shadowbox or picture frame

Glue

White card stock

Old rag or cloth

Small paintbrush

Black paint

Metallic spray paint

Keys

How to make

Start by laying out the keys and selecting the ones you want to use. Then gather your materials, among them an old or inexpensive frame or shadowbox to fit your keys. You can color your keys gold or silver. You only need to paint one of the sides as the other will be glued down.

If you want to give your keys a vintage look, you can dab black paint all over them, using a small brush and making sure it gets into the crannies and nooks. Then gently wipe away the paint, using a piece of old cloth and leaving some behind in the recessed areas.

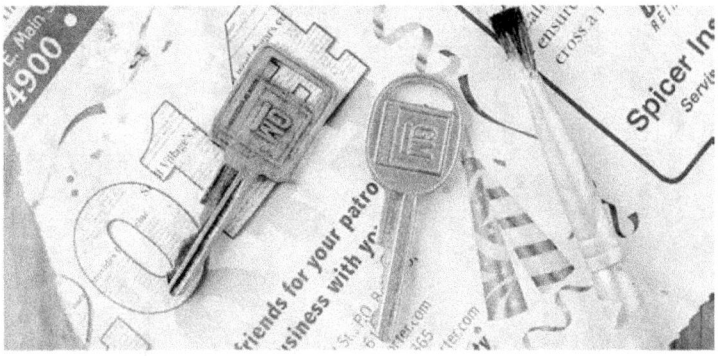

Start with just a little paint and immediately wipe it before you add more coats. Repeat the painting and wiping until you get the look you're after.

Allow the keys to dry and then prepare to frame them. Attach a piece of white cardstock to the interior side of your frame backing and glue your keys onto the paper. Using a paintbrush, apply enough glue to ensure the keys remain in place, but be careful not to have it spread all over.

For a more elegant look, use a black frame as well as an ivory mat.

Reupholster a chair

What you'll need

Fabric

Staple gun

Chair with cushion

How to make

Position the fabric over the seat and then cut it out. Leave a few inches allowance on each side. You can either cover over the original fabric or remove it and make an all-new cushion.

Now pull one of the edges of the fabric around the sides and then use a staple gun to staple every few inches around the border. When you're finished with one side, repeat for the other side, pulling the fabric tight. Do the same for the remaining two edges.

Now pull the fabric straight up from the corners and push it down to create a smooth edge. Hold the fabric with one hand and staple it with the other. Cut off any extra fabric and put the cushion back onto the chair.

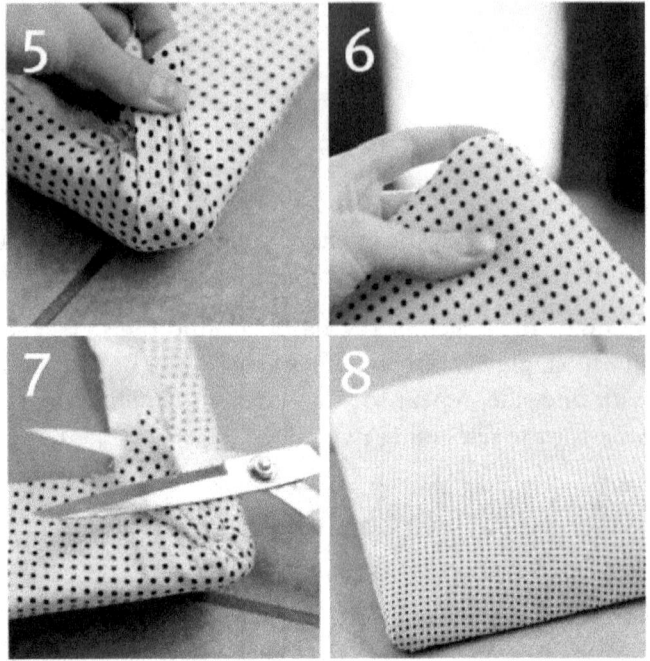

DIY Faux Headboard

What you'll need

Paint and a paintbrush

Gorilla glue

Screws and a drill

Spray adhesion product

Fabric of your choice

1-2 large frames

Wood cut to fit the frames

How to make

Obtain two 26x38" frames. According to the size of your bed, measure the inside of the frames and deduct about an inch vertically and horizontally. The two boards will serve as a backing for your headboard.

Lay your boards on the underside of your chosen fabric. Trace using a yellow marker and cut your fabric to fit the boards. Use spray glue to join them.

Allow time for the glue to dry and then attach the boards to the frames using glue and small screws. For polish, you can use silver acrylic paint. To paint the frame, use a stencil brush and then wipe it off. Allow the paint to dry and then test by hanging on your bed.

DIY Fabric Art

What you'll need

Nails or command strips

Hammer

Hot glue

Fabric

Frames

How to make

Decide the size of your frames depending on where they're to be used. Remove the cardboard from the frames and then tape it to the wall. This shows you how the frame will appear on a wall so you can choose the spacing for different frames.

Cut about 1/8" off the edge of the cardboard to make room for the fabric when you put it in the frame. Now cut out a fabric piece that is 2 inches wider than the cardboard, wrap the cardboard the way you'd wrap a gift, and hot glue it. Place the piece in the back of the frame.

You're finished already, after less than an hour of work! Now you can hang your new fabric art for you and your guests to admire.

Chapter 2:
Homemade Crafts, Clothes and Accessories

Reusable Lunch Bags

What you'll need

5 inches of Velcro

6x3" main and lining for flap

6x15" main and lining

How to make

Start by cutting your fabric to the above measurements, or to your preferred size. Make sure the fabric is about ¾" wider than the finished size and twice the finished height. Also, leave ¾" for seam allowance. Start by cutting one piece of lining and one piece of main fabric. Then cut a piece of the main and lining for the flap, ensuring the flap pieces are similar in width to the bag pieces, and also 3 inches high.

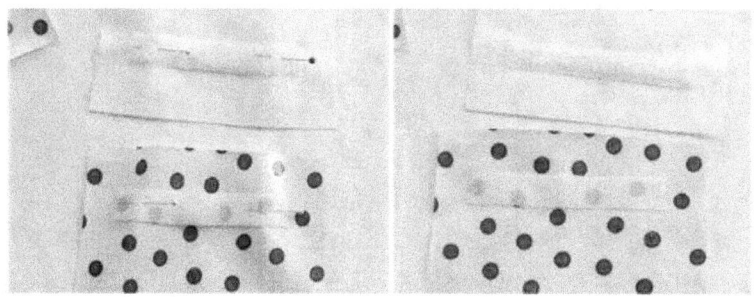

Now attach the Velcro by sewing the rough piece about an inch down the edge of the main bag piece, centered on the exterior side. Then sew the soft piece of Velcro about an inch from the edge of the lining flap piece, which is centered on the right hand side of the fabric.

Now sew the flap into place by putting the two right-side flap pieces together. Sew around three sides, leaving about ¼" of seam allowance and leaving the top edge open. To round the corners, trace a round object and then sew along the curved lines. Then trim the corners together with the seam allowance. Turn your flap right side out and set aside.

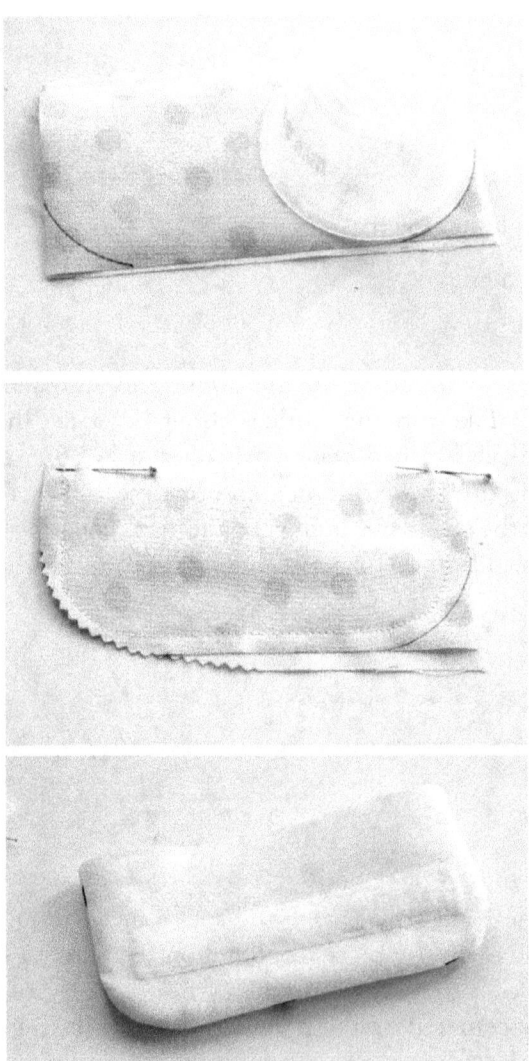

As shown above, sew the two pieces together to make pockets. Work on the main bag piece together with the lining of the bag piece separate, and fold the bag in half lengthwise. Ensure the right sides are facing each other. Stitch down each of the sides, backstitching both at the beginning and the end to secure your stitches. When finished sewing, trim the bottom corners.

To stitch the pieces together, press the seams of the lining pocket flat, and turn it right side out. Then slip the lining pocket into the main pocket, with the right sides in. Match the side seams. Put a couple of pins along the top edge, but make sure the pin holes won't show in the finished oilcloth. Then insert the flap piece, fitting the lining pocket between your two pieces of Velcro, which should be facing each other. Match the raw edges for the pieces at the top.

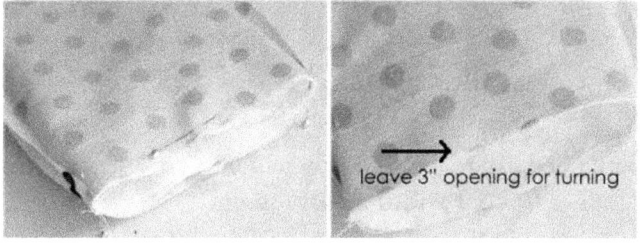

leave 3" opening for turning

Use a ¼" seam allowance to stitch all the way around the edge of the pocket. Also, leave an opening of about 3-4" at the center, on the opposite side that has the flap.

Slowly turn the project right side out, taking caution not to tear or damage the oilcloth. Then push the lining into place as the interior side of the bag. Fold the raw edges of the opening in then press them in place with your fingers.

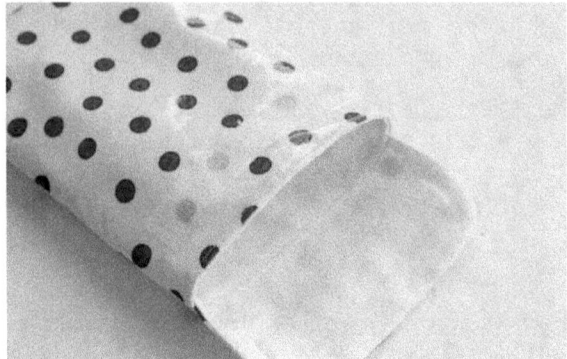

Finally, top stitch around the bag to give it a finished appearance and close the opening. If desired, you can press the top of the bag before you stitch, pressing the lining only using a cool iron. You may also turn the bag to have the lining face out in case your sewing machine cannot pull through the oilcloth. You are now set to use your bag.

In case you need to make a sandwich bag or add extra room, add another 2 inches to your width measurement.

DIY Mason Jar Soap Pump

What you'll need

Glue gun

A pump from an old dispenser

Pretty paper to jazz up your jar

Jar lid

Mason jar

How to make

In the center of your lid, drill a hole big enough to fit the bottom portion of your pump. Use a glue gun on the bottom of the lid to make a seal between the soap pump and the lid of the jar. This step helps to keep the lid from rusting. You're now ready with your pump gift.

Mason Jar Cozies

What you'll need

2" piece of sew-on Velcro

12.5x3.5" piece of insulated batting

2 pieces of fabric, 12.5x3.5"

Sewing machine and basic supplies

How to make

Gather your materials, cut them to size, and then pin the fabric to the batting. The order of pinning should be layer and pin, then insulated batting, fabric right side up and finally right side down. Ensure you leave about 3-4 inches of gap for turning later on.

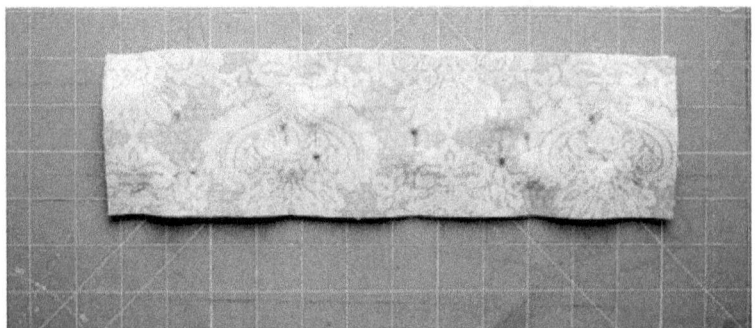

Using a ½" seam allowance, sew around the edge, carefully pivoting at the corner. Leave an opening to backstitch later. When done with sewing, remove the pins and then clip all four corners of your fabric. Do not cut too close to your stitching.

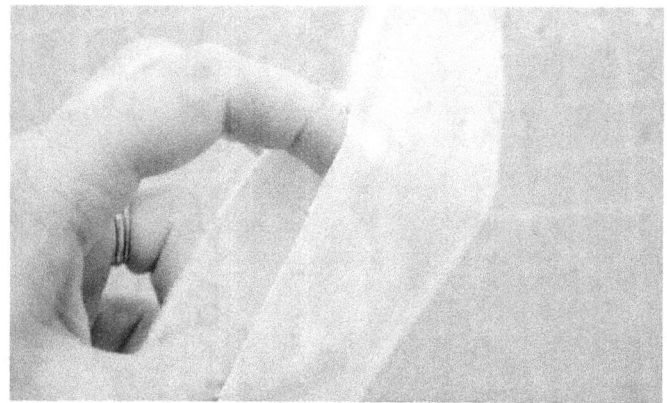

Now turn the cozy inside out and use your knitting needle to push out the corners very carefully and press. Fold in the opening to ensure that the seam resembles the other stitching.

Now top stitch using a seam allowance of ¼" around your entire cozy, ensuring the opening you previously left is sewn shut. Pin the Velcro pieces after you're done with the stitching.

Pin one side of the Velcro to the back of the cozy and the other to the back so it closes completely around your jar. You may need to test whether it fits properly. Sew as close as possible to the edges around each piece of Velcro.

Now trim away any loose threads to complete the Manson jar cozy, and you have your gift ready.

Mesh beach bag

What you'll need

Sewing machine

Scissors, thread

Hole punch

Rivets to attach handles

Leather strip for handles

15 cm zipper for the zippered pouch

Bias tape

A piece of oilcloth, to make a zippered pouch and cover the board

A piece of plastic for the bottom, 13x51 cm

Window screen material, 66x100 cm

How to make

Cut the following sizes from your fabric or oil cloth: 1 rectangle, sized 17 x 28 cm, and 1 rectangle, sized 17 x 6 cm.

Attach one side of the zipper, ensuring that the zipper faces the right side of the smallest piece of your oilcloth. Fold it over and top stitch, repeating this for the other zipper half together with the largest rectangle. Do a top stitch.

Fold the fabric over to make a pocket and then close the side seams onto the right side, about ½ centimeters from the edge. Complete the seam using a bias tape and then repeat the operation for the other side seam. Close on the right side and cover using the bias tape. You don't have to sew the top of the pocket closed as it would be absorbed into the top hem of the bag.

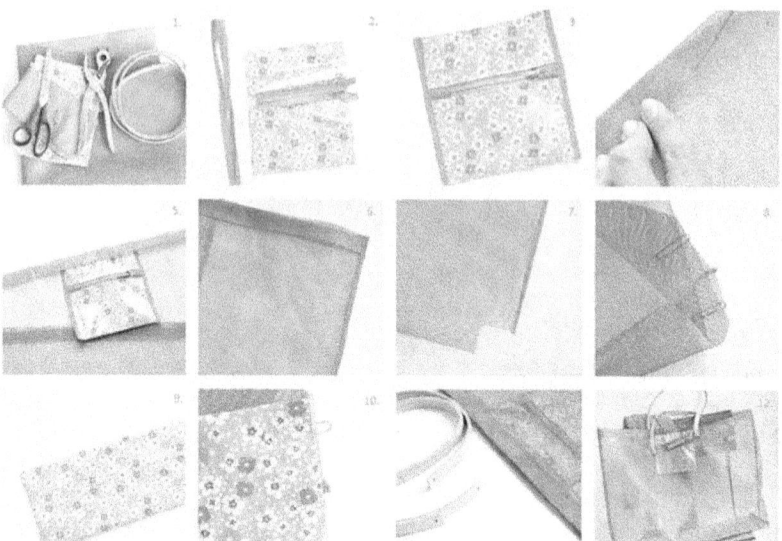

To assemble the bag, follow this tutorial for the different parts:

Top hems: Fold about 3 centimeters at the short end of the window screen material and then fold over a second time. If needed, use a bone folder to make a crease and then secure using paperclips. Now top stitch to join into lace and repeat this at the short end. However, ensure that you incorporate the zippered pouch and center it nicely. Use paperclips to secure it and then top stitch into place.

For the side seams: Start by folding the screen material into half, with the right sides facing. Close the side seams, about ½ centimeters from the edge. Using fabric bias tape, carefully bind the side seams.

For boxed corners, sew them in place. Consider pre-cutting the boxed corners to avoid sewing through too many layers. You may also cut away the excess materials after you're through with the boxed corners. Just cut away a square that has sides equal to the width of your panel when halved, in case you're going to cut before you sew the boxed corners. But ensure that you consider the seam allowance.

Bag bottom stabilizer

For this, make a cover for the oil cloth to use in the plastic bag stabilizer. Sew two pieces of oil cloth together that measure the size of the board but with a 1-centimeter allowance on all sides. Just leave one of the sides open, and then turn over and insert the board.

To join the stabilizer to your bag, arrange the open end with the boxed corners and then sew together. Use the fabric bias tape to bind the seams together and bind the other boxed corner. You should attach the plastic board to one side of the bag only.

Handles: Before joining the handles, you need to determine where to fix them and then punch the required holes as desired. Make holes both on the handles and bag and then use rivets to attach. Include a small piece of leather in the back to ensure that the rivets match the thickness of the materials you use. This gives your bag a strong and durable handle.

Simple hair bow tutorial

What you'll need

Scissors

Hot glue

Hair clips

Ribbon

How to make

Cut the ribbon; it should be 5-6 inches, or longer depending on the size of the recipient of your gift. Then fold in one end up to the center and join using hot glue. Fold the other end to meet the first ribbon in the middle and apply just a little glue. Put a small dot of glue onto the center of your bow and then pinch together.

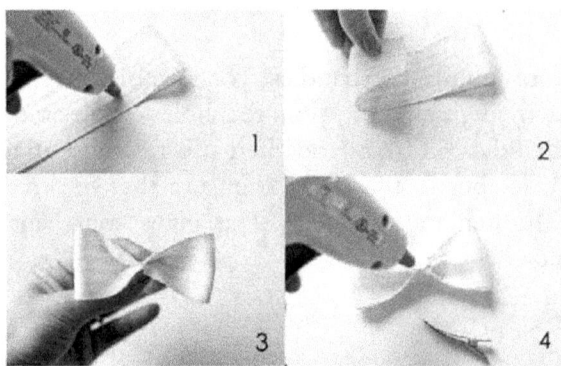

Next, pull the ends back and glue a ½" piece of the ribbon around the center. You can cut a ½" piece from your ribbon or use a ribbon in another color. Ensure the edge doesn't fray by using fire or a fray check. Finally, glue the alligator hair clip onto the ribbon and you are done!

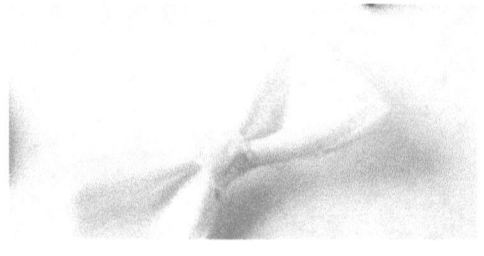

Chapter 3:
Summer Food Gifts

Decadent Brownie Pie

What you'll need

2 cups walnuts, chopped

3 tablespoons milk

½ teaspoon salt

1 ¼ cups all-purpose flour

2 eggs

½ cup light corn syrup

½ cup baking cocoa

1 ¼ cups sugar

2/3 cup butter, softened

For the Ganache:

8 (1-ounce) squares semisweet chocolate, chopped

1 cup whipping cream

How to make

To prepare the brownies: cream butter and sugar in a mixing bowl and then add in corn syrup. Beat in eggs one at a time and mix cocoa, salt and flour in a separate bowl. Add this dry mixture into the creamed mixture alternately with milk before folding in the walnuts.

Now spread the mixture into a greased 10" pan and bake for about 55-60 minutes at 325 degrees F. When ready, a toothpick inserted into the brownie should come out clean. Cool the brownie on a wire rack.

To make the ganache: bring cream to a boil in a saucepan. Then remove from the heat and stir in chocolate until melted.

Once the brownie has cooled completely, put the wire rack over some wax paper. Pour the ganache over the brownie and spread it over the top, allowing it to drip down the sides. Allow it to stand until set and then cut it into wedges. You can garnish with your preferred toppings or store in the fridge. This is an amazing dessert to serve your guests.

Mint Chocolate Cake

What you'll need

1 cup mints, chopped

1 teaspoon vanilla extract

½ cup oil

1 cup sour cream

2 eggs

2 teaspoons baking soda

1 teaspoon baking powder

1 teaspoon salt

¾ cup cocoa powder

1¾ cups flour, all-purpose

2 cups granulated sugar

1 cup boiling water

For mint butter-cream frosting

½ cup milk

Green food coloring

1 teaspoon peppermint extract

1 teaspoon vanilla extract

6 cups confectioner's sugar

1 cup (2 sticks) butter, unsalted

For chocolate ganache

1 teaspoon vanilla extract

1 cup heavy cream

1 cup chocolate chips, semi-sweet

How to make

Preheat your oven to 350 degrees F. Line 8" cake pans with wax paper and then grease the sides of the pans. Bring water to a boil inside a small sauce pan and let it simmer as you combine the other ingredients.

Whisk together salt, baking powder, baking soda, cocoa, flour, and sugar in a mixing bowl. Then add in vanilla, oil, sour cream and eggs, and use an electric beater to mix the contents completely.

To the mixture, add a cup of boiling water. Stir the mixture gently until fully combined. Use the electric mixer to beat the contents for about 1½ minutes.

Put the chopped mints and a tablespoon of flour in a Ziploc bag. Shake completely to coat the mints with flour, then fold them into the batter. Transfer the batter into prepared pans and bake for about 20-30 minutes. Then insert a toothpick into the center to see if it comes out clean.

Prepare the mint butter-cream frosting by creaming some butter into a large bowl until fluffy. Add in a few cups of sugar one by one, and combine well. Now mix in the food coloring, peppermint and vanilla, and then add milk slowly to attain your desired consistency. Keep the contents covered.

Make the chocolate ganache by putting some chocolate chips into a small metal bowl. Over medium heat, heat some cream and monitor it closely. Then remove from heat immediately it starts to boil. Pour the cream over the chocolate chips and allow to rest for about 1-2 minutes. Stir the mixture slowly to completely melt all the chocolate before you stir in the vanilla.

Let the ganache chill and thicken by allowing it to stand at room temperature for a few hours. You can also refrigerate it to make this process faster. Pour the ganache over your cake, spiraling gradually outward from the center. Cover any unused portion and refrigerate for not more than two weeks.

Creamy Garlic Mushrooms

This is an amazing recipe that you can prepare for guests or give to a host when visiting over the summer.

What you'll need

1 teaspoon of olive oil

Salt & pepper

1 teaspoon of herbs, fresh or dry

2 tablespoons of cream cheese

2 cloves of garlic, minced

8 ounces of mushrooms, whole white

How to make

Heat a teaspoon of oil in a pan over medium heat. Add in the mushrooms and garlic, then stir and toss until soft. This should release some liquid from the mushrooms, but if it doesn't, add a few tablespoons of broth or milk.

Add in the cream cheese and mix well. Follow this with herbs such as tarragon, basil, and parsley, then season with salt and pepper. Ensure you don't overheat to prevent the cheese from splitting. You may choose to first remove from heat as you add the cream cheese, then mix well and heat gently until the sauce bubbles and heats through completely.

When done, serve the mushroom straight from the pan, or put into an oven dish and store covered to keep warm.

Chapter 4: Miscellaneous Summer Gifts

Cute button bookmarks

What you'll need

Felt

Hot glue

Fancy buttons

Paperclips

How to make

Start the project by hot gluing a paper clip onto the back of a button. Next, cut out a little piece of felt to fix at the top. The felt should ensure that the glue is sealed in and that you achieve a smooth finish.

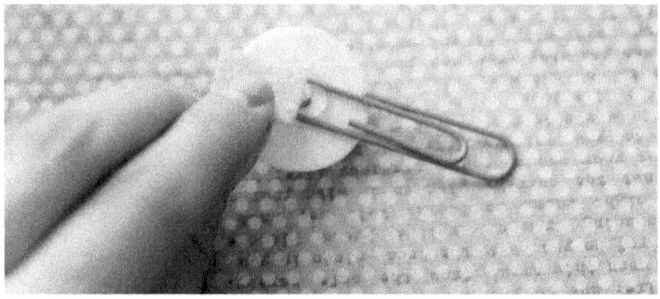

You can explore different fun button styles to make your summer gift unique.

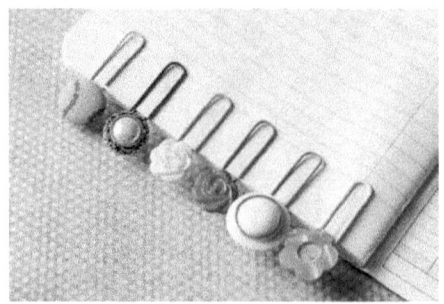

Homemade Sandcastle Kit

What you'll need

Painter's spatula

Measuring cups and spoons

Funnels

Brushes

How to make

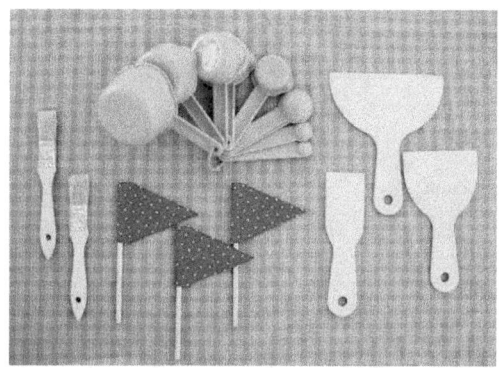

You need a painter's spatula to help you carve the sand into smooth sides, walls and stairs. The spatula also allows you to level the sand.

You also need brushes for getting the sand out of the cracks and plates. And of course you need flags! You can make a flag from a double-sided fusible interfacing, fabric and a wooden dowel.

Bubble solution and blowers

What you'll need

Tape

Straws

12" pipe cleaners

Bottle or container

Light corn syrup

Liquid dish soap

Water

For bubble solution

½ cup liquid dish soap

½ cup light corn syrup

2½ cups hot water

How to make

Into hot water, add about ½ cup of corn syrup and whisk until well combined. Slowly add in ½ cup of liquid dish soap and whisk completely. Pour the bubble solution into a container with a lid or a bottle. Allow the solution to cool for a couple of hours.

Line up a couple of straws and then wrap them around using tape to make up bubble blowers. Make the bubble wands by bending pipe cleaners around different shapes such as cookie cutters. Then wrap the remaining wire around the stick portion to keep it in place.

When you're ready to blow bubbles, you can transfer the solution into jars for each user. You can re-use your plastic cups, jars or yogurt cups with lids for this.

Conclusion

Handmade gifts are unique and demonstrate your love and affection much better than store-bought products that anyone could buy. Even better, most of these gifts are inexpensive and easy to make when you follow the directions and pictures provided in this book. Even if you're not an artist or artisan, it's very easy to adopt these ideas to make unique gifts. Just obtain the raw materials listed and you are good to go.

Key Takeaways from this Book

- This DIY book presents various gift ideas that can be made using readily available and affordable materials.

- The book is designed to help you save money by turning otherwise useless raw materials into creative DIY gift ideas. It's time to utilize some of the items that you don't use to come up with amazing gifts.

- By following the tutorials, you can design unique and presentable gifts regardless of whether you have experience. The ideas are easy to learn and carry out.

- You now have a variety of ideas to try out to explore your level of creativity. These ideas are all designed to be understood and implemented within a few hours.

How to Put This Information into Action

1. Start by seeing which materials you have and how much it would cost to buy the ones you don't. Think about how much time each project will require and plan efficiently.
2. Consider the intended recipient of the gift. You need to design and present gifts that make sense to the recipient.
3. Evaluate your technical skills before you venture into making handmade gifts to avoid damaging materials or starting projects you can't complete. While you are bound to make mistakes as you start, try to practice on inexpensive materials until you get it right.
4. Think about how to make your gifts different this year. For instance, you may want to offer food gifts if you presented homemade craft gifts last year.

Here's another book you might like:

Preview of DIY Projects & Gift Ideas for Easter:

Amazingly Easy Guided Gift Ideas For Beginners To The More Experienced

Chapter 1: Easter Eggs Gifts

1. Easter eggs that glow in the dark

What you'll need

Candy

Tape

Glow Sticks

Plastic Easter Eggs, large or medium

How to do it

Snap glowing sticks and then insert them into the plastic eggs together with candy. Tape shut and you have your glowing Easter Eggs.

2. Washi Tape Easter Egg Wreath

What you'll need

All-white plastic eggs

Washi Tape

Wreath Form

Hot glue

Ribbons

How to do it

Obtain a wreath form and then wrap it using bright pink ribbon. Wrap the eggs using washi tape, starting from the base of the egg. Pull the tape very firmly as you wrap it around the egg. Use your fingers to smooth the wrinkles appearing on eggs.

To stick the eggs onto the wreath form, use hot glue and then add pinwheels and ribbons to the front.

3. Easter note eggs

What you'll need

Vinyl or stickers

Dye Kit

Hard-boiled eggs

How to do it

Boil the eggs and allow to dry. Design your vinyl and then cut, peel and add adhesive to the vinyl. Add vinyl to the eggs, making sure that they are firm enough when pressed.

Put the eggs in dye cups according to instructions on dye kits. Let them to set for some time, then pull out and allow to dry. Peel of the vinyl, to see the messages that are left on the eggs.

4. Easter Egg Planters

What you'll need

For Planting Wheat Grass

Kitchen scissors/gardening shears

Egg crate

Organic soil

Wheat grass seeds

For The Egg Shell Planter

Painter's tape or Electric Black Tape

Egg shells in halve

Vinegar

Scrap booking puncher of your desired shape

Food colors (different colors)

Freezer paper or used sticker paper backing

To plant wheat grass

Only pick the whole grain shape seed for planting. Get rid of any broken pieces, which may rot and kill the wheat grasses. Soak the healthy seeds in filtered water for 24 hours, ensuring that the water covers the seeds.

After a day, drain the water and then rinse the seeds, and ensure to pick any broken seeds. Now put dump towel over for about 8 hours to facilitate sprouting. Prepare a sowing ground for the seeds (you can use a polyfoam). Place a kitchen towel onto the sowing ground then spread the seeds evenly.

Cover the seeds with a thin layer of organic soil. After planting, wet the soil regularly three times a day and place the bowl or in our case the egg crate in a place that it receives sunlight. Your wheat grass will be ready in 8 days.

How to Prepare Easter Egg Planters

Plant the wheat grasses in the egg crate about 5-7 days before you make the egg planter and allow them to grow at the windowsill for a few hours of exposure to sunlight.

Prepare the eggshell planter that you would use. Divide the eggshell in half; gather various food colors and vinegar. Make a stencil sticker by sticking the electric black tape on the shiny side of the freezer paper. Using your favorite puncher, punch out the shape you would like. Peel the freezer paper from the tape then attach it to the egg halve. Press all sides to ensure that it is set nicely.

Prepare your dye by adding 10 drops of food color to ¼ cup warm water. You can have different colors depending on the amount of food color you use. Dip the eggs into the dye and leave them for some time. The longer you leave them the darker the color. Remove them then place on pin board to dry. Once the eggshell has dried, peel off the sticker and wait for the wheat grass to grow to maturity.

Cut your egg crate, separate the wheat grasses and then trim the egg crate to make it fit into an eggshell.

Position the wheat grass into the eggshell by squeezing the crate a little to comfortably fit the egg shell.

The wheat grass should last for about a week, then cut the grass and allow it to grow again. If you prefer longer lasting Easter planters, you may opt for little herbs such as thyme and rosemary.

5. Moss covered Easter eggs

What you'll need

Scissors

Buttons

Twine

Plastic Eggs

Hot Glue Gun

Moss

How to do it

As the project is a little bit messy, you need to put something under your work area to minimize the dirt falling on you. Tear some moss pieces and then shape it to fit an egg.

Apply hot glue to the eggs and then press the moss in place, and continue to fill the holes up until you have covered the eggs with moss. If gaps exist, take some pieces falling off, add glue, and then press into these gaps.

After all gaps are filled up and your egg is fully covered, take the scissors and cut the stray mosses. However, do not throw away the clippings, as you would need them for filling in gaps on other eggs.

If desired, you may add twine by wrapping around the egg then add a dot of glue on the button and stick onto the moss.

6. Washi Tape Eggs

What you'll need

Hard-boiled eggs

Dye

Washi tape

Bunch of rolls of glitter

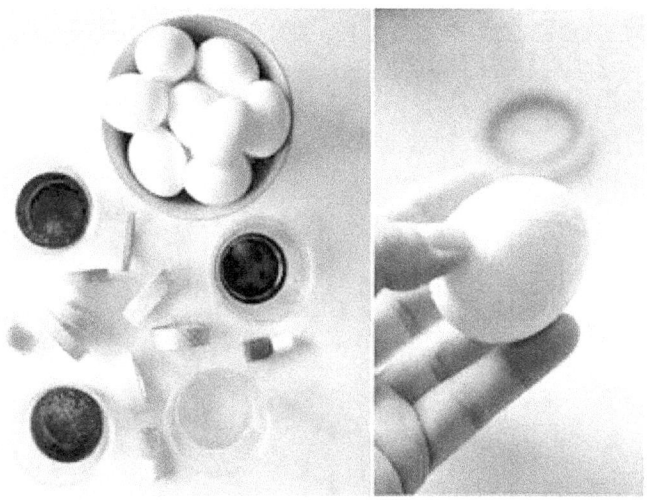

How to do it

Create a banded pattern by wrapping washi tape on your hard-boiled eggs. Dip the eggs into your dye, dry them and then peel the tape to reveal the pattern.

To make a spotted design on the eggs, use nail polish and then dip into a dye. Make a number of applications to get the best appearance.

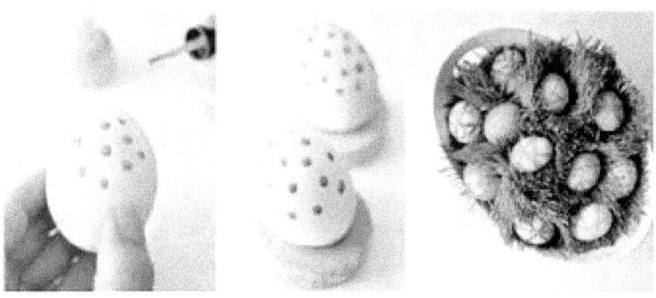

Nest them into grass that is inspired by traditional Easter egg hunt if desired, such as wheat grass. You might also like to throw some chocolate candies.

**To Download The Rest of This Book
Copy & Paste To Your Browser The Link Below:**

http://www.amazon.com/DIY-Projects-Gift-Ideas-Easter-ebook/dp/B00TRWJRKQ

More Books You Might Like

Household DIY: Save Time and Money with Do It Yourself Hints and Tips on Furniture, Clothes, Pests, Stains, Residues, Odors and More!

DIY Household Hacks: Save Time and Money with Do It Yourself Tips and Tricks for Cleaning Your House

Essential Oils: Essential Oils & Aromatherapy for Beginners: Proven Secrets to Weight Loss, Skin Care, Hair Care & Stress Relief Using Essential Oil Recipes

Apple Cider Vinegar for Beginners: An Apple Cider Vinegar Handbook with Proven Secrets to Natural Weight Loss, Optimum Health and Beautiful Skin

Body Butter Recipes: Proven Formula Secrets to Making All Natural Body Butters that Will Hydrate and Rejuvenate Your Skin

Kindle Unlimited Subscribers Can Read All These Books for Free!

Click Here for More: *http://amzn.to/1bRDHH9*

If the links do not work, for whatever reason, you can simply search for these titles on the Amazon website to find them.

Your Free Bonus

As a way of thanking you for your purchase, I'm offering you an opportunity to sign up and be a part of an exclusive book list where members get advanced notice on high-quality books.

To be part of this exclusive club, click on the link below:

https://docs.google.com/forms/d/1ttDqtdRjOeAEtA-BKnq5Hw668vjQS0VWcXCGQ8z9frA/viewform

www.ingramcontent.com/pod-product-compliance
Lightning Source LLC
Chambersburg PA
CBHW072209100526
44589CB00015B/2448